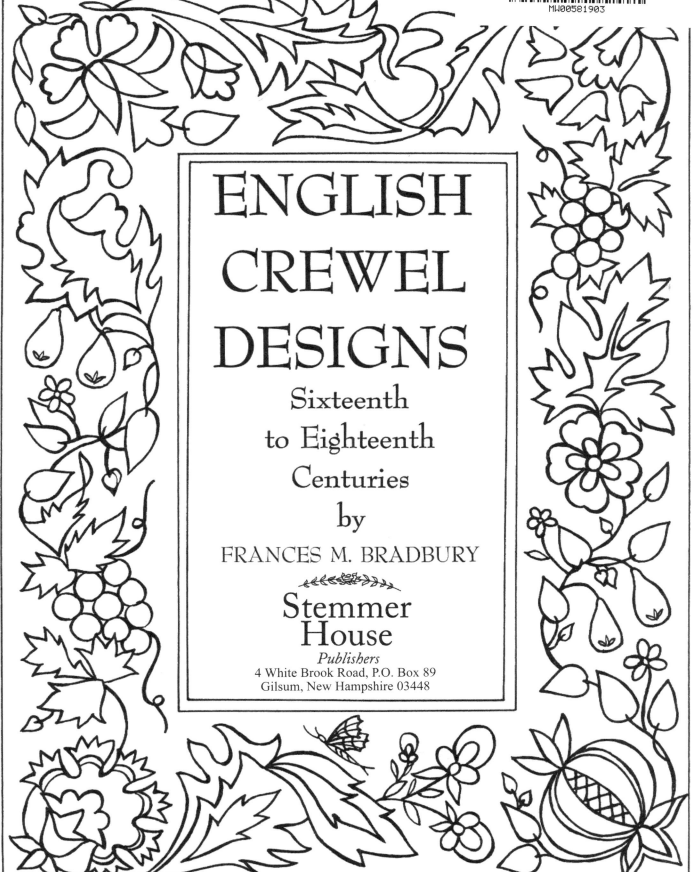

ENGLISH CREWEL DESIGNS

Sixteenth
to Eighteenth
Centuries
by

FRANCES M. BRADBURY

Stemmer
House

Publishers
4 White Brook Road, P.O. Box 89
Gilsum, New Hampshire 03448

Introduction

THE TERM "CRUELL" originally referred to a particular kind of twisted, or worsted, wool. In later years the term came to mean a decorative embroidery worked with colored wools and called "crewel" embroidery.

One of the oldest embroideries to have survived the vicissitudes of time is the famous Bayeux Tapestry. Worked with colored wools on a bleached linen ground, the tapestry, 230 feet long and a bit less than twenty inches in height, features seventy-two scenes of the Norman Conquest of England in the year 1066.

During the reign of Queen Elizabeth I (1558-1603), there was greater political stability, with improved economic and social conditions, factors which made it possible for secular and domestic embroidery to flourish. Prior to this time, and especially between the mid-thirteenth and mid-fourteenth centuries, professional English embroiderers, both men and women, produced ecclesiastical embroideries of such superb quality that this needlework became famous throughout Europe. Known as *Opus Anglicanum,* these embroideries were rich in design, decorated with jewels and silver and gold thread.

With the arrival of the Elizabethan era, the great demand for ecclesiastical embroideries greatly declined, while, with the emergence of a growing, wealthy middle-class, a tradition of domestic embroidery arose.

Luxuries were no longer just for the nobility. Townhouses and comfortable country houses, surrounded by gracious gardens, were built to meet the new demands. Household furnishings large and small, personal clothing and accessories, all were enriched with decoration. The gardens received extraordinary attention and care, for during this era a good deal of social entertaining was done there, with people participating in musical events and dancing.

In noble households a professional embroiderer might well have been a member of the staff, for there was much work to be done keeping embroidered furnishings and clothing in good repair. Additionally, the professional created new designs for the mistress of the household. Many long hours were spent daily at embroidery tasks.

Lesser households saw the rise of the skilled amateur needlewoman and the flourishing of domestic needlework. The bed, a four-poster of huge proportions, was the major household item and held to be of great value. It had from four to perhaps six curtains, which when pulled together, formed a complete enclosure for the occupants within. The richest materials were used; imported silks, linens, velvets and brocades. The curtains, valances, coverlets, pillows, pillow covers and chair cushions provided the needlewoman with an opportunity for much creative embroidery. Introduction of the steel needle, and its availability, aided in the accomplishment of beautiful needlework.

Personal clothing and accessories for both men and women received close attention. Among the many articles which received embroidered decoration were jackets, coats, waistcoats, caps, coifs, dresses, smocks, petticoats, stomachers (triangular shapes, which filled in the bodice-fronts of dresses), gloves, mittens, purses, pockets, small bags, book covers, military scarves, and in later times slippers, shoes, and short aprons. England was famous for its beautiful wools, which were inexpensive and easily obtained by the embroiderer. The imported silk threads were so costly that they were sometimes combined with the wools for certain embroidered pieces.

Blackwork embroidery, said to have been introduced to England by Catherine of Aragon, first wife of King Henry VIII, was particularly favored by Elizabethans. Black yarn worked on a white ground resulted in stitchery patterns resembling lace. With a heavy tax on it, lace was very expensive, and so collars and cuffs were decorated with blackwork. Household items, too, such as cushions and curtains, received similar embellishment.

The extent of embroidery opulence can be clearly seen in portraits of royalty or members of the court, who posed for paintings of themselves during this era. Royalty set the example, with nobility and the gentry emulating the current fashionable styles.

Queen Elizabeth, herself a needlewoman with a special love for embroidery, granted the first charter in 1561 to the Embroiderers' Guild. During her reign she received many magnificent gifts of embroidery from her court, important diplomats and visitors.

Embroidered in a naturalistic way, the following were favorite subjects appealing to the Elizabethan needlewoman:

Flowers: Carnation, tulip, rose, daffodil, pansy, primrose, honeysuckle, thistle, daisy and cornflower. Also, the pea pod and the acorn.

Herbs: Rosemary, thyme, rue and lavender.

Fruits: Strawberries, pears, grapes and pomegranates.

Animals: Rabbit, squirrel, lamb, fox, deer, and larger animals like the unicorn, lion, leopard and elephant. And all manner of crawling insects, flying insects and birds.

Applique was another method of embroidery. Small panels were separately worked on canvas. When finished, they were then appliqued to a larger background of velvet, thereby creating a sumptuous total effect for their decorative hangings. Table and floor carpets were also worked on linen canvas, adding greater warmth and richness to the household.

The sampler at this time was used to record patterns and stitches the embroiderer wished to remember for further use. In later years, during the seventeenth and eighteenth centuries, samplers became full embroideries in their own right, receiving greater detail and elaboration. Many samplers were created and worked by very young girls.

With the advent of printing there were far more design resources for the embroiderer. Books were imported from France, Italy, Germany and Flanders. In England, "The Schole-House For The Needle," by Richard Shorleyker, published in 1624, was immediately popular, and it was reprinted in many succeeding editions. An earlier book of 1597, "Gerard's Herbal," complete with descriptions and woodcut illustrations of the many plants known at the time, was another popular design resource. So too, was John Taylor's book, "The Needle's Excellency," published in 1634.

Engravings, paintings, books on natural history, garden books, the Bible and classical and mythological stories and characters furnished more material for the needleworker. In addition to pattern books, single sheets and collections of patterns, prepared by the professional designers, were printed and sold.

The floral scroll with its coiling, twisting stem enclosing flowers, leaves or fruits, was typically Elizabethan, not found in other European embroidery. The single flower or sprig was also used, and at times the single flower became an all-over pattern for a costume. On occasion, flowers, insects, animals and birds were arranged in rows, embroidered with much imagination and highly stylized.

The familiar patterns repeated endlessly in embroideries not only appeared on textiles, but were used to decorate unrelated objects such as furniture, silver and ceramics.

With the establishment of the East India Company during the reign of Queen Elizabeth, trade with India and China brought new influences. Imported fabrics rich in color and design gave fresh inspiration to the embroiderer. New, exotic flowers and birds, combined with those long familiar, gave added interest and impetus to English embroiderers.

In the early years of the seventeenth century, spice ships returning to Britain with their cargoes also carried with them a small lot of hand-painted Indian cottons. There was an immediate market for these chintzes and palampores, and the demand for them grew. They were made up into dressing gowns, petticoats, dresses, curtains and quilts.

The Tree of Life, with its strong Near East influence, was a favored embroidery theme. The tree was placed on, or arose from, a series of hillocks or earth mounds. Floral sprigs, garden insects, and animals large and small were interspersed amongst the little hillocks. This embroidery was especially enjoyed, for it provided the needleworker with much opportunity for individual expression.

The method used for dyeing and painting the India cottons permitted the rich and brilliant colors to remain fast, rather than fading with use. By the mid-seventeenth century, through trading companies such as the East India Company, English pattern makers were sending out their designs to be copied and painted on Indian fabrics and then shipped back to them. Since the flowers of the English garden and countryside were unfamiliar to the cotton painters, the designs in translation received unusual treatment, bearing in their final painted state a mixture of Indian, Chinese and European influences. Once returned to England, these painted cottons in turn became a further source for embroidery inspiration.

The bed still remained the most important article of furniture. There was a move away from heavy velvets and brocades for bed hangings and curtains. A linen and cotton mixture, having a twill weave, that was imported from India became a preferred fabric for crewelwork. There was a taste for bed hangings embroidered with assymetrical patterns of curving stems and spreading branches adorned with large, bold leaves and flowers. Embroidered with wools, the color schemes were often monochromatic, with much use of greens, blues and browns. A variety of stitches might include the outline or stem, chain, herringbone, back stitch, long and short, coral, French knot, laid and couching stitches.

Along with crewelwork, stumpwork and embroidered pictures were in vogue. Stumpwork involved a method of embroidering over raised forms, giving a relief effect, and was used to decorate trinket and jewel boxes, little cabinets and mirror frames. Themes for embroidered pictures included portraits of reigning royalty and designs copied from larger woven tapestries; and from the Bible, the Garden of Eden gave great scope for imaginative embroidery. Perspective and proportion were not a major concern despite the great attention given to even the most minute details. Fruits, flowers, leaves, nuts and even people appeared in disproportion to one another.

Chinese influences became more prominent as the eighteenth century advanced and "Chinoiserie," an English term, came into use. Professionals and amateurs alike copied the novel exotic designs, with their bright colors, from the imported fabrics, tapestries, wallpapers and lacquer work. Little garden scenes were embroidered with all manner of pavilions, strange rocks, bridges, fences, temples and oriental figures, appearing along with the old favorites—the rose, carnation and tulip.

Crewelwork curtains and bed hangings continued to be embroidered with more brightly colored wools on a white ground. The tree designs of earlier times were now more slender in form, embroidered with many Chinoiserie motifs. Floral borders became more important and were frequently part of a coverlet design, including the very popular quilted ones.

Costumes continued to be embroidered with floral patterns and brilliantly colored silk threads. More and more furniture was covered with canvas work embroidered with pastoral landscapes and hunting scenes, or upholstered with the more available imported fabrics.

Towards the end of this era, however, the quality and quantity of embroidery declined. With greatly increased trading, beautifully woven and printed fabrics were replacing the areas of decoration that in earlier times required the skills of the embroiderer; and the Industrial Revolution also made its contribution to the continuing decline of the craft of embroidery.

F.M.B.

BIBLIOGRAPHY

Beck, Thomasina, *Embroidered Gardens*. New York: Viking Press, 1979.

Beer, Alice Baldwin, *Trade Goods*. Washington, D.C.: Smithsonian Institute Press, 1970.

Connoisseur Period Guide: *Tudor Period* 1500-1603 vol. 1; *Stuart Period* 1603-1714 vol. 2; *Early Georgian Period* 1714-1760 vol. 3; edited by Ralph Edwards and L. G. G. Ramsey. New York: Reynal & Company, 1957-1958.

Digby, George Wingfield, *Elizabethan Embroidery*. London, Faber & Faber, Ltd., 1963.

Drysdale, Rosemary, *The Art of Blackwork Embroidery*. New York: Charles Scribner's Sons, 1975.

Gibbs-Smith, Charles H., *Bayeux Tapestry*. London: Phaedon Press, Ltd., 1973.

Jones, Mary Eirwen, *A History of Western Embroidery*. New York: Watson-Guptill Publications, 1969.

Kendrick, Albert F., *English Needlework,* second edition revised by Patricia Wardle. London: Adam & Charles Black, 1967.

Schuette, Marie and Müller-Christensen, Sigrid, *A Pictorial History of Embroidery*. New York: Frederick A. Praeger, 1964.

Swain, Margaret H., *Historical Needlework, Scotland and Northern England*. New York: Charles Scribner's Sons, 1970.

Wardle, Patricia, *Guide to English Embroidery*. London: Her Majesty's Stationery Office, 1970.

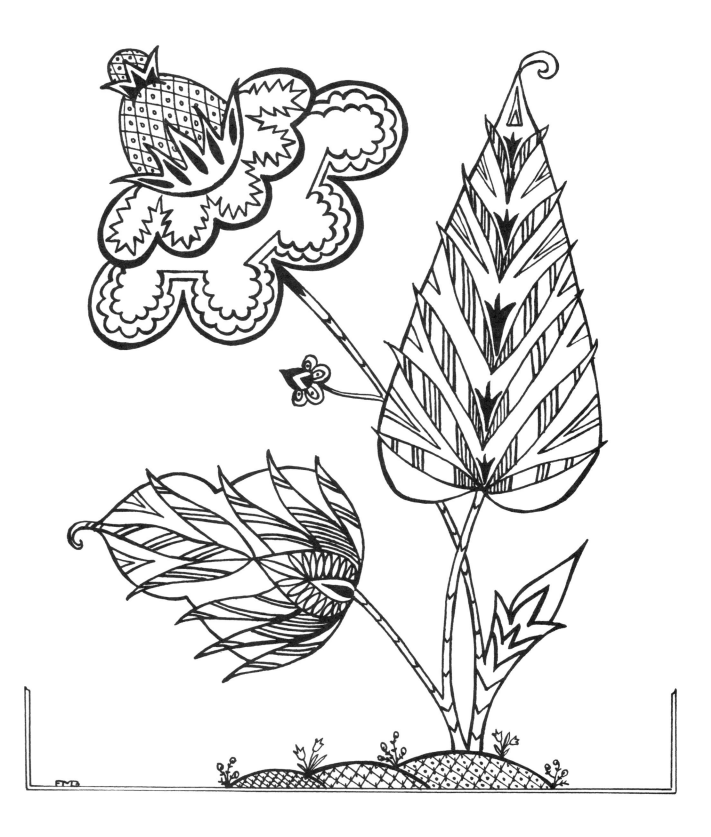

Designed by Barbara Holdridge
Composed by the Service Composition Company,
    Baltimore, Maryland
Printed and bound by Cushing-Malloy, Inc., Ann Arbor, MI